Using Pinterest For Your Family History & Genealogy

MELISSA DICKERSON,
GENEALOGY GIRL TALKS

ISBN: 1533348405
ISBN-13: 978-1533348401

COPYRIGHT

This book is dedicated to my son, Thomas, with love.

CONTENTS

ACKNOWLEDGMENTS

I wish to personally thank the following people for the contributions to my inspiration and other help in creating this book:

You know who you are! Every person who I have shared my dreams with and who has showed interest in helping me pursue my dreams, thank you! Your kindness and encouragement has pushed me forward. I could never repay each of you. Perhaps, a simple "Thank you!" will suffice.

1 STARTING WITH THE BASICS

Have you ever considered using Pinterest for your Genealogy and Family History research? I started using Pinterest for my Family's Genealogy and I love it! It is a great way to organize the family photographs and documents you find around the internet. Plus, as an added bonus, the link to the document and family photo is provided and you can easily share them with family!

There's no need to save old family photographs to your computer (and forgetting the source). And there is no more taking other people's photographs and posting them as your own. Now, with the assistance of Pinterest, you can simply share them through what Pinterest calls a "pin".

So, if you have never been on the Pinterest website or you are not too certain what all this Pinterest "talk" is about, let me explain it in simple terms. After all, Its a good idea to start with the basics and build on that, right?

What is Pinterest?

I like to think of Pinterest as an online image search engine. It's a lot like Google, Bing, and Yahoo, but with a twist. Once you type in your search words your results are displayed as images and pictures. This can be very helpful for those who do family genealogy. Imagine the surprise when your ancestor's picture shows up and it is a photograph you've never seen before! Plus, there is a link attached and you can click to see both the photo and the website where that image is stored.

However, before we get started, lets first look at a few terms (with definitions and an explanation) related to Pinterest:

Pin: This is basically the image that you "pin" to your boards. Yes, the term "pin" is both a verb and a noun. It is the image itself and the act of placing the image on your board.

Boards: These are where the pins you pin are placed. They are a way to organize your pins. Many people on Pinterest have multiple boards, but you don't necessarily need a lot of boards. My husband, for example, actually only has one board that he pins everything to. Personally, I like to keep everything organized and I have many boards. Keep in mind, it is all personal preference. Do what works best for you! I have seen some pretty extensive boards on Pinterest. I remember searching and finding one user who creates board covers for each of her boards. It is really eye catching and I'm sure others remember her boards, too. I have seen another user who color coordinates all of her boards, too. She has board cover images that are color coordinated. I love this idea, too!

Pinning: This is the process of adding a pin to one of your boards. Usually this is done through the "Pin It" button. You don't always need to use the "pin it" button to pin to your boards, you can upload images (pins) directly to Pinterest, too.

Pinner: This a term used to describe all of us Pinterest users! Yep, its true! Did you know you are a "Pinner"?

Repin: This is the process of pinning another pinner's pin. See what I did there? I was checking to make sure you understand the above terms. Okay, enough fun and games, basically, when you repin another user's pin, it is called a repin. This is the fun part of Pinterest and what keeps this platform going. Oh, and its also fun to see your own pins get repinned.

Liking: The act of liking another user's pin. To like a pin, you simply click the heart icon on the pin. Liking is not the same as pinning. The pin doesn't appear on your boards, but it will appear on your list of "Likes" that other users can see. Some people like more than they pin and other users pin more than they like. Once again, it is personal preference.

Following: Following on Pinterest is very similar to other social media platforms. The difference is that you can follow all of a user's boards or you can simply follow only specific boards. When you view another Pinner's boards you can see which boards of theirs you currently follow. You will see the words "follow" in red if you are not following that board and the words "unfollow" in gray if you are currently following the board.

Follower Count: While this is not the most important part of Pinterest, it does need a definition and explanation. Your follower count on Pinterest includes the number of people who are following your boards. This includes those who follow only 1 board and those who follow all your boards. Recently, I started following at least one board of those who follow me. After all, we need to keep the

Pinterest Train going, right? On a side note, If you follow me and I didn't do this, give me time, I'm going through and correcting this.

Pin Description: This is the text area that you use to write the description of your pin. It can be as long or as short as you prefer. You can edit this area on pins you are repinning, too. I like to add a little bit more information on my Pin Descriptions. I usually add something that will benefit my followers. Also, if you are interested in SEO and optimizing your pin for searches, add some searchable keywords here, too. This is a great place to add Family Surnames, Dates of Birth, Dates of Death, locations, and more from your Family History and Genealogy. Oh, and you can add hashtags (#) here, too! If you have a blog or website, you can add that information to the pin description, too.

Direct Messaging: Recently (August 2014) Pinterest added the Direct Messaging feature to their platform. For a long time there was a "comment" section under each pin, but this was very public. Now, Direct Messaging allows you to send pins and direct messages (or both) to other users. To use this feature, just click on the little paper airplane looking icon.

Now that you have the basics of Pinterest down, you are ready to get started!

Lets Get Started with Pinterest

The first step to getting started on Pinterest is to set up an account. This is a rather simple process. First, head over to www.pinterest.com and join. You can create an account with your Facebook, Twitter, or with just your email.

Once you set up your account you can add information to your profile, add a picture, and add a description. These areas are not required to be completed, but it will help others find and follow you. I suggest completing each section as thoroughly as you can. For example, on your description add the Surnames of the families you are researching. Do you have a family history blog? Add your website to your Pinterest profile! People (and family members) will be able to find you easier if you include correct and purposeful information in your profile.

Now that you have your account and you set up your profile, its time to create your boards. After all, your pins need a place to be stored! To create boards, simply click the "+" sign to add your board. Give it a title, place it in a category, add a description, and decide if you want your board to be "secret" or public. Be sure to complete the board description. This will, once again, allow others to find you and your boards through the search feature.

You can also create Secret Boards on Pinterest. What are these boards, you ask? Secret boards are boards that only you can see. You can make them public later if you prefer, but remember that boards that start out as public boards can not be made secret at a later time. I will explain some suggestions for using these secret Pinterest boards for your Family History & Genealogy in a later chapter.

Now, that you have an account and are all set up in Pinterest, lets look at the many benefits of using Pinterest for your Family History and Genealogy...

2 BENEFITS OF USING PINTEREST FOR YOUR FAMILY HISTORY

There are many benefits to using Pinterest for your own family history and genealogy. Pinterest is a great platform for connecting with family, researching your own family, organizing the information you find, and so much more! The possibilities are endless.

Let's look at a few benefits to using Pinterest...

Organize Your Information

Pinterest gives you a great way to organize your information and pins. Each user organizes their pins on boards. These boards can be as broad or as specific as you like. You create them and you decide how to organize them.

In the last chapter I discussed how to create boards, but lets look at how to organize your boards.

In this example, I will explain how I created and currently organize my genealogy boards. In the beginning, when I first joined Pinterest, my boards were a mess! But, in time, I began to organize them in a more effective way. A few of the boards I currently have are:

- Genealogy Girl Talks *(this is my website and podcast board)*
- Genealogy & Family History
- Crafts DIY - Family History & Genealogy
- Family History Quotes
- Genealogy 101 - Learn How
- Family History Organization
- WV Genealogy
- Fraysier (Frazier) Family Genealogy
- Hager & Goodman Family Genealogy
- Scott County Virginia
- and more.

I also have boards of personal interest to me like

- Healthy Recipes
- Smoothie Recipes
- Coffee Love
- My Style and Fashion

As you can tell, I like to pin... a lot!

My boards are a variety of topics and I name them while keeping keywords in mind. After all, I want to assist others in finding my boards (and pins) while they are searching. How you organize your boards is completely your personal preference. To organize your boards pick different categories. Use those categories to name your boards.

Connect With Family

I believe a very important key to doing Genealogy & Family History research is connecting with family. I have had so many great experiences just by reaching out to family online. I've found family I didn't even know I had! Emails, online family trees, Facebook, Twitter, and even Pinterest all offer ways to connect with family!

A great way to connect with family (and other users) is using Pinterest's Direct Messaging feature. I described this feature in a previous chapter, but Direct Messaging isn't the only way to use Pinterest to connect with family.

Family can find you just by simply pinning your pins! For example, the next time you are doing your family history research and you come across an amazing website related to your family, pin it! Pin it to one of your Family boards and now someone researching the same family can find you (and your pin, of course). Don't forget to add information to the pin description to help others find it in their search.

I know, from my own experience, that creating Family boards (surname boards) help to get your family involved. If you are known as the family historian and your family loves when you share information, send them to your Pinterest board! I shared information on my Family Board and once the word got out, I had family (that I didn't even know) start following my board. Its really exciting!

Save Pictures & Documents

As you are searching the internet and come across some amazing information, you can pin it to your boards. Many websites now offer a "Pin-it" button that easily pins to your boards with a few clicks. Simply click the "Pin-it" button, select an image from the choices that pop up, choose which board you would like the image to be pinned, and you are all set!

Once your pin is pinned, the link (URL or source code) is saved and the next time you want to go back to that website, just click on the image and you will be taken there.

Pinterest is a great bookmarking tool. Remember the days of saving websites to your "Favorites"? Now, you can pin them and save them to your boards - with images!

There are still some websites that do not have the "Pin-it" button, but there are templates you can use (see Chapter 5 for more information). Also, many web browsers allow you to use a browser based "Pin- it" button. These are available through Pinterest's website. They are a great tool.

3 CREATIVE WAYS TO USE PINTEREST FOR FAMILY HISTORY

I have been a member of Pinterest for a while. Just like you, I've pinned recipes, quotes, inspirational items, information on medical conditions, exercise, health, and so much more! It never occurred to me that Pinterest is a great tool for Family History and building my Family Tree.

I love to search Pinterest for genealogy related pins. I've found inspiring craft and DIY ideas, ideas for displaying family photographs, printable family trees, resources for researching my ancestors, and a lot of ideas for my next projects. I have seen a lot of amazing and creative ways people are using Pinterest and how they are organizing their boards - some have even brought tears to my eyes.

I want to share a few of the creative ways others are using Pinterest and, hopefully, inspire you with ideas on how you can create your own family history and genealogy boards on Pinterest.

Keep in mind that these are just a few ideas I came up with. You can create your boards (and use Pinterest) any way you want! I would love to see how you choose to use Pinterest for your family history.

Memorial Boards

Many of these types of boards have brought me to tears. I've seen others with boards titled "Things my Father loved", "Places Mom visited", and "Grandma's Garden". I've spent a lot of time looking through these boards, of complete strangers, but felt connected in some way. Memorial Boards are a beautiful way to create a Memorial for your family member and ancestor.

How can you create Memorial Boards for your ancestors? You can pin images of your ancestor's favorite things. What were their favorite types of food? What were their favorite flowers? What were their favorite places to visit?

Places Boards

A few ideas for Place Boards are places your ancestors lived or came from, history of the state or county your family lived in, cemeteries your ancestors are buried, and so much more.

My family came from Germany, Scotland, England, Ireland, and more. It would be a great idea to build a board on Pinterest filled with pictures and links to the towns, cities, countries, and landmarks that your family came from. If you are like me, you may never travel to these countries, but now you can, through images and pictures.

You can also find information online (and even within Pinterest) related to the history of the state, county, or towns your ancestors lived. My family is mainly from Virginia, West Virginia, Kentucky, and Ohio. I have a few boards related to the area my ancestors lived in Virginia and West Virginia. I also have a board dedicated to the history of the county my family lived. I find it fascinating to learn the history of this area!

Objects, Dress, Ways of Living

What a wonderful way to portray your family heritage! Create a board based on the occupations of your ancestors. Were they farmers, coal miners, or bankers? What types of tools and machinery did they use during that era? What did they wear? Another idea is to create a board with pins related to the dress and apparel of your ancestors. There are beautiful images of clothing from the 1800's available.

Family Surname Boards

Another great way to use your Pinterest boards is to create Family Surname Boards. These will help others who are researching the same surname to find you and your pins.

Family Surname boards are a great way to organize information you found online and keep it all in one place. While you're researching on the internet, look for the "pin it" button and add the website to your boards.

You can even pin pictures, Find A Grave Memorials, cemetery information, court records, census images, and more to your boards. Anything you find online can be pinned to your boards!

These are just a few ideas of the numerous (and creative ways) you can build and name your boards on Pinterest. The possibilities are endless!

4 USING PINTEREST TO CONNECT WITH FAMILY

If you are currently using Pinterest for your Family History & Genealogy there was a feature added in August 2014. I was so excited when I heard they added Direct Messaging to their platform. It is available on both the desktop and mobile apps.

What does this mean? It means that now you can message other Pinterest users! Now, I'm not talking about spamming people, but I am talking about connecting with family!

If you are familiar with Genealogy Girl Talks then you know that I believe connecting with family is a key element in doing Family History and Genealogy. There is so much information available from family members if we just ask. Sure, some family members do not want to talk or they say the don't know anything, but if you keep connecting you will find one who will turn your world upside down with the information they share with you!

Imagine all the potential cousins out there! Why not attempt to connect with them?

How do you use the Direct Messaging feature on Pinterest, you ask? It's easy to do, whether you are on a mobile device or a desktop.

1. Log into your Pinterest account. If you don't have a Pinterest account, it's easy to set up. Go to: www.Pinterest.com and sign up. All you need is an email address.
2. After you log in, you will see a few icons. The house icon is your home screen (or main feed). The magnifying glass is where you will search. The text bubble icon is where your notifications are located. This is where you will find the Direct Messaging feature. The fourth icon is a person sign. This is where you can view your profile, your boards, pins, add pins, and so much more!
3. Click the "text bubble" icon. You will see three options at the top of the screen. They are labeled "News," "You," and "Messages." If you click News you will see what the people you follow have pinned, boards they now follow, and other items. The You tab is where you will see your own notifications. The Message tab houses your direct message.
4. Click the "Messages" tab near the top of your screen (on a mobile device). You will see your messages, if you have any, here. This is where you will compose and receive your messages. Are you ready to send Genealogy Girl Talks a message? Let's try it!
5. In the center of the screen you will see a red circle with a "+" symbol in the center. Click this icon.
6. The next screen will prompt you to enter the recipient of your message. Enter "Genealogy Girl Talks" or any other Pinterest user. You can also enter an email address here.
7. Click the next button.
8. If you look at the bottom of your screen, you will see a

text box with "Add a message." You can begin typing your message here. If you wish to send a "pin" to someone, you can click the little plus symbol and pushpin icon to the left of the text box.

9. Begin typing your message, then click the send button. Now, your message has been sent!

5 HOW TO PIN IMAGES

An important part of using Pinterest is pinning images. There are several ways to pin images to your boards. Whether you are using the desktop version or a mobile device, the process of pinning images is quite similar.

The majority of Pinterest users use a mobile device of some kind. The general information I will give here will help both mobile and desktop users.

The easiest way to pin an image when you're browsing the internet is to look for the "Pin-it" button most websites display. Some websites have the button near the top of the page, some display the button when you hover or tap an image, and many blogs have a list of "share buttons" near the bottom of their articles and posts.

If you find a "Pin-it" button on the website you are viewing, click on it. Images you can select from will pop up on your screen. Click the image you would like to pin to your boards. Pinterest will allow you to select the board to pin the image onto. Before you click the board, check the pin description (near the top of the screen) to verify the text located there. You can make changes to the pin description, too. Once you are happy with the pin description (you can add the website name and link here if you want), select the board, and your image has been pinned.

After I pin an image, I like to go back to the board I pinned it onto. I make sure everything looks good, the link works, and the description is accurate. You can add keywords into the pin description to help others find it, too.

If the website you are viewing doesn't have an actual "Pin-it" button, you can still pin the website to your board. It's a little trickier to do it this way, but with a little practice and repetition, you will be a pro in no time!

To pin an image this way, copy the website address (or URL). To copy it you can drag your mouse over the entire text and click CTRL+C on a Windows device or CMD+C on an IOS device. You've now copied the link to your "clipboard."

Now, head over to your Pinterest account. Look near the top of the page and you will see a plus ("+") symbol. Click on this. Several options appear: Create new board, Photos, Location, Clipboard, and Web. Since you copied the website's address to your clipboard, click that.

Pinterest will open up its browser with the website address that you copied. It will then select an image for you to pin. Click on the image, and the same information, as above, appears. Before you click the board, check the pin description (near the top of the screen) to verify the text located there. You can make changes to the pin description, too. Once you are happy with the pin description (you can add the website name and link here if you want), select the board, and your image has been pinned.

You can also pin your own pictures and images stored on your computer or mobile device. Follow the same procedure as above (click the plus "+" sign), but this time you will select Photos. Pinterest will ask you which photograph you would like to pin. Select the image and follow the screen prompts to pin your picture. Be sure to add a pin description prior to selecting a board.

The following chapter in this book describes how to use Templates for pinning information you find online. Some websites don't contain images and Pinterest will not allow you to pin an all text webpage. The workaround I found was to create Templates. When you pin your Templates, you follow the same procedure for pinning one of your photographs as stated above.

If you want to use Pinterest's browser feature to find images to pin, you would simply follow the steps above (click the plus "+" sign) and select "Web." This will open the browser. You can enter a website and search the internet for images this way. The same steps for pinning, as stated above, apply.

Now, you are familiar with pinning images to Pinterest. It is the best part of Pinterest. The more images and pins you add, the more robust Pinterest grows! Go out there and help your favorite websites and blogs by pinning their information. It really helps their readership and follower numbers grow!

6 USING TEMPLATES

Okay, so we've all done it. All family genealogists have done it at some point. We've found photographs of our ancestors, saved them to our computers, and shared them to family without linking to the proper source (or even giving credit to the person who owns the photograph), right?

This, my friend, is bordering on copyright infringement and I know that I am not alone in this. I am not an attorney (nor do I pretend to play one on the internet or in books), but I believe I have a "system" that will assist many of us who dance around the awful "copyright infringement" line and will prevent us from crossing that fuzzy gray area.

Want to learn more?

In my genealogy and family research via the internet, I have encountered many photographs of my ancestors, census records, biographies, cemetery photographs, and more. These are not my own personal creations - I didn't take the pictures or create the documents. I don't have the copyright on these either.

Therefore, am I allowed to create screenshots of them, copy and save the image to my own online tree or computer, or even "pin" them to Pinterest without a link? What if the website I found them on doesn't have a "pin it" button - which in a way says "go ahead and pin it", right?

This is that gray area of copyrights and it creates many to question it.

So, how do I do it?

For me, personally, I do not seek out disobeying copyright laws. My intention is not to steal your photos or take your documents. When I use Pinterest and pin these images, I want to share these with other family members, not break laws.

If there is not a "pin it" button on the website, I typically will use a pre made templates that I created. I use a photo editing program that allows me to overlay text on these templates. They, I upload (or pin) this image to my boards and edit the source link to direct anyone who click on the image to the website where I found the photograph or document I want others to see.

All that may sound complicated, but once you do it a few times, you will see how easy it actually is.

Below is an example of a Pinterest Template I use:

The following picture shows the text overlay that I added to the pre-made Pinterest Template. This is the image I uploaded (or "pinned") to Pinterest.

When this image is clicked, it links to a free online record of the 1940 census that includes my ancestor listed above.

This image was pinned using the procedures mentioned in this book, however, in order to link this image to the correct source I had to go into Pinterest and edit the "source" for the image. You can edit the source (or link) for any image you pin by selecting the "edit" button for the image. It is a small pencil icon.

7 PLANNING AHEAD

Before you dive into creating your Pinterest account, pinning, and creating boards, it's a great idea to plan ahead. There are a few questions to ask yourself before you get started. I put together a list of those questions (with space for you to write your responses) to help you prior to beginning your journey.

This helpful guide will assist you as you begin your journey:

Question	Response
What username will you use? Your username will be part of your Pinterest web address (URL). For example: www.Pinterest.com /yourusername	

Question	Response
What do you want to name your account?	
Which email address will you use to create your account?	
Will you link your Facebook or Twitter account to your new Pinterest account?	
What types of boards do you want to create? Memorial boards? Place boards? Surname boards? Or other boards?	
If creating Memorial boards, how will you use them?	
If creating Place boards, which places and locations will you use?	
If creating Surname boards, which family surnames will you include?	

Question	Response
Will you use a Templates to pin and link to websites?	
Where will you store and save your templates?	
What graphic program (or app) will you use to create your templates?	
Notes:	

These are just a few questions to ask yourself before you begin your new Pinterest for Genealogy journey. There is a blank area for your to add your own notes and any information you may need before you begin.

8 NOW IT'S TIME FOR YOU TO GET STARTED

Lets see, now you know what Pinterest is and the basic terms associated with it. You know the Benefits of using Pinterest for your Genealogy & Family History. You are aware of how to use Templates for your pins and the importance of connecting with family. Well, it looks like you are ready to get started with using Pinterest for your family's Genealogy & History research.

I offered you many tips, tricks, and advice throughout this book, but its time for you to take the first step and create your boards and start pinning!

I can't wait to see what you create and how you use Pinterest for your own Family History & Genealogy!

Let me know how it goes!

I would love to see your boards, too!

You can contact me at genealogygirltalks@gmail.com

9 BONUS: 10 TIPS FOR USING PINTEREST FOR GENEALOGY

I put together this short little list of 10 tips to help you use Pinterest for your Family History and Genealogy. It is filled with brief tips to help you in this journey!

Keep in mind that there is no right or wrong way to use Pinterest for your Family History. The beauty of Pinterest is that it is completely customizable and you can tweak it as you go!

I hope these 10 Tips help you as you begin to use Pinterest for your Family History & Genealogy!

1. Pinterest is a Search Engine.

Keep in mind that Pinterest is considered a search engine. Keywords and searchable terms are necessary to be found. How can you use these keywords? Place keywords such as Family Surnames in the pin description of your pins. This will help others find you!

2. Complete your Profile.

Be sure to completely fill out your Pinterest profile. Complete your "About Me" section to assist others in finding you! Remember to use keywords (see above) in your description. If you have a blog or website, add that information to your profile, too!

3. Consider using Templates.

Keep in mind that if a website has a "pin it" button they are giving you permission to use and "pin" their images to Pinterest. On the flip-side, if they do not have a "pin it" button they are technically not giving permission to pin their images. Now I know there are a lot of websites that do not understand Pinterest, or the importance of using Pinterest, but to comply with copyrights consider using a Template for images and links to websites.

4. Pin it & Share.

Did you know that you can share your pins on other social media sites? Facebook, Twitter, and more allow you to integrate your pins. Consider using these to share your pins (and help others find you).

5. Use the Direct Messaging Service.

This is a new service offered by Pinterest and I believe it is a valuable tool to connecting with family!

6. Comment on Pins.

Commenting on pins can start a conversation! You never know the family you will meet just by commenting!

7. Follow others.

This is a mistake I made in the beginning of my Pinterest journey: I didn't follow others. Now, I've learned the importance of following other "pinners". I don't follow so they will "follow me back" but I follow to find more pins for my own boards!

8. Fill in your Board Descriptions.

Your board descriptions help people find your boards on Pinterest. Remember Pinterest is a search engine and users can search for information by boards. You want to make sure your board descriptions are completed and contain keywords (or search terms) that others will use to find you!

9. The more the merrier.

In my own journey using Pinterest for Genealogy I have found that the more pins on a board, the more views I receive. I'm not sure how this happens, but for some reason it does. So, I would suggest that you fill your boards with a lot of quality pins!

10. Check The Link.

How do you check the link of your pins? A simple "click-through" will check the destination URL (or website) of the pin. This will help your followers! Do you want to send your followers to a spammy website through one of the pins you pinned to your boards? Take a quick second to make sure the pin sends people to the correct website.

11. BONUS TIP #1:

Make sure the pin description is filled out! I've seen many users that simply have a "." or the words "love" as their pin description. This will make it difficult for your pins (and you) to be found on Pinterest. Take a moment to fill in the pin descriptions located under the pin.

12. BONUS TIP #2:

Use the Secret Boards that Pinterest provides. There are several ways to use the Secret Boards. For example, when you are creating a new board and you only have a few pins added you can create a secret board to fill up and then make it visible to others. Or you can add pins to your secret board and then repin them to a public board. Consider using your Secret Boards - they can really come in handy!

13. BONUS TIP #3:

Remember that the order in which you pin your pins is the order they appear on your boards. Does that sound a little confusing? Basically it means your older pins are at the bottom of the board and the newest ones are at the top. If you want a few of your pins to appear together on your board, consider using the Secret Boards and then repin them to your public board in your predetermined order.

THIS PAGE INTENTIONALLY LEFT BLANK.

ABOUT THE AUTHOR

Melissa Dickerson, also known as "Genealogy Girl Talks" has been conducting family history and genealogy research for over twenty years. She has a love of history, family, teaching, and creativity. Those four passions pushed her to create Genealogy Girl Talks in 2014.

She wrote her first eBook, "10 Tips for Using Pinterest for Family History" in the Fall 2014. That was followed by several more quick tip eBooks. In May 2016, her first print book was self-published ("Using Pinterest for Family History and Genealogy").

Melissa lives in Northeast Ohio, but her roots find her deep in pursuit of her family history in Appalachia. Her burning desire to learn more about her family and her roots in Southwestern West Virginia has quickly become her life's pursuit.

www.ingramcontent.com/pod-product-compliance
Lightning Source LLC
Chambersburg PA
CBHW062023280526
45787CB00005B/2206